North West England Vol II
Edited by Mark Richardson

 Young**Writers**

First published in Great Britain in 2007 by:
Young Writers
Remus House
Coltsfoot Drive
Peterborough
PE2 9JX
Telephone: 01733 890066
Website: www.youngwriters.co.uk

SB ISBN 978-1 84431 137 8

Foreword

Young Writers was established in 1991 and has been passionately devoted to the promotion of reading and writing in children and young adults ever since. The quest continues today. Young Writers remains as committed to the nurturing of poetic and literary talent as ever.

This year's Young Writers competition has proven as vibrant and dynamic as ever and we are delighted to present a showcase of the best poetry from across the UK and in some cases overseas. Each poem has been selected from a wealth of *Little Laureates* entries before ultimately being published in this, our sixteenth primary school poetry series.

Once again, we have been supremely impressed by the overall quality of the entries we have received. The imagination, energy and creativity which has gone into each young writer's entry made choosing the poems a challenging and often difficult but ultimately hugely rewarding task - the general high standard of the work submitted ensured this opportunity to bring their poetry to a larger appreciative audience.

We sincerely hope you are pleased with this final collection and that you will enjoy *Little Laureates North West England Vol II* for many years to come.

Contents

Jessica Hill (11)   37
Lois Kershaw (11)   38
Lauren Evans (10)   39
Niall Murphy (10)   40
Eleanor Graham (11)   41
Edward Cleary (10)   42
James Cleary (10)   43
Nicholas Whittam (10)   44
Melissa White (10)   45
Kelsey Caldwell (9)   46
Sinead Mooney (8)   47
Daisy Metcalfe (9)   48
Molly Lawton (8)   49
Aiden Murray (8)   50
Mariah Clenkian (9)   51
Kieron Jones (9)   52
Georgia Croman (8)   53
Matthew Harold (9)   54
Carl Whittam (8)   55
Molly Johnson (8)   56
Jasmine Taylor-Sharp (8)   57
James Orwin (9)   58
Paige Clayton (9)   59
Ross Murray (10)   60

St Kentigern's RC Primary School, Blackpool
Conor Lunn (10)   61
Hayleigh Smith (9)   62
Ben Campbell (9)   63
Samantha Smith (9)   64
Chelcee Starkie (10)   65
Daisy Lonsdale (9)   66
Joseph McMahon (10)   67
Anthony Platt (10)   68
Alex Houldsworth (10)   69
Aria Kiely (9)   70
Emma O'Mahoney (10)   71
Emma-Nicole Mansfield (9) & Katie O'Connell (10)   72
Aimee Morrissey-Hill (10)   73
Ivan Villarino (9)   74

St Leonard's CE Primary School, Preston

Katherine Foweather (8)	75
Priya Manivannan (9)	76
Rebecca Jack (9)	77
Danyelle Hodgson (9)	78
Ben Hargreves (9)	79
Rhys Massaro (8)	80
Alex Calderbank (8)	81
Daniel Lawler (8)	82
James Robinson (9)	83
Oliver Cuerden (9)	84
Bradley Reid (9)	85
Karl Riley (9)	86
Genavieve Borg (9)	87
Matthew Davis (9)	88
Asha Nayli (9)	89
Clara Butler (8)	90
Luke Wilson (8)	91
Emily Brown (8)	92
Phoebe Child (8)	93
Harriet Devine (8)	94
Harriet Smith (8)	95
Emma Kulbacki (9)	96
Alex Sahillioglu (9)	97
Niall Riley (8)	98
Thomas Hampson (9)	99
Shelby Preston (8)	100

St Paul's RC Primary School, Blackburn

Jenny Parker (10)	101
Howard Livesey (10)	102
Adam Burgess (10)	103
Ben O'Ryan (11)	104
James Jackson (10)	105
Chloe McGrath (10)	106
Jenna Parkinson (11)	107
Eleanor Rawstron (11)	108
Charlotte McManus (10)	109
Anna Moorman (10)	110

St Peter's CE Primary School, Bolton

Alex Tudge (8)	111
William Lee (8)	112
Rebecca Townsend (9)	113
Matthew Wills (8)	114
Georgina Kilmartin (9)	115
Kirsty Green (10)	116
Amy Tudge (10)	117
Abigail Cooper (9)	118
Molly Fitton (9)	119
Jessica Wonta (8)	120
Joe Madden (9)	121
Teejay Jackson (8)	122
Rebecca Larkin (9)	123
Daniel Brabin (9)	124
Courtney Jackson (8)	125
Kai Belk (8)	126
Bethany Greenhalgh (9)	127
Rachel Wolstencroft (9)	128
Aaliyah Westhead (9)	129

Stamford Park Junior School, Altrincham

Katie Mullings (8)	130
Anna Cooper (8)	131
Chanelle Burke Robinson (7)	132
Louise Scotson (8)	133
Philip Owen (7)	134
Amy Mather (7)	135
Mollie Axon (8)	136
Katy Cai (8)	137
Rosie Peachey (7)	138
Sadie Tully (9)	139
Emma Davies (9)	140
Lottie Peachey (9)	141
Helen Cohen (9)	142
Chloe Knowles (9)	143
Julia Madeley (9)	144
Euan Gilchrist (8)	145
Ava Mullen-Cooper (9)	146
Allicia Birch (8)	147
Molly Harrison (9)	148

The Poems

My Poem

Ears as big as a blanket,
Eyes as big as the moon,
Trunk like a pole,
Head like a ball,
Legs like tree trunks.

Demi-Lea Wall (8)
St Dominic's Catholic Junior School, Liverpool

My Poem

Feet as small as nails,
Head as small as a pea,
Eyes like buttons,
Teeth like knives,
Tail as long as a snake,
Skin like burnt toast.

William Johnson (9)
St Dominic's Catholic Junior School, Liverpool

Love

Love is kind,
It is not easily angered.
Love is calm, it forgives.
Love feels special,
It smells of fresh roses.
Love tastes like lovely chocolate,
My tummy turns over with excitement.
Love never ends.

Ellie Shacklock (9)
St Dominic's Catholic Junior School, Liverpool

Darkness

Darkness is like a spider, as black as coal.
Darkness is like a weird mixture stirred in a dark bowl.

Darkness is the sound of thunder and silence.
Good overcomes evil but darkness is violence.

Darkness is the smell of ashes so black.
Darkness is so bad it could give you a flashback.

Darkness feels like a bat poisoning me.
Darkness is as painful as the sting from a bee.

Darkness looks like pitch-black smoke.
Darkness is so bad it could make you choke.

Saffron D'Arcy (9)
St Dominic's Catholic Junior School, Liverpool

Laughter!

The colours of laughter are just so bright,
I just cannot deny, they are *brighter* than bright,
They are like the sun in the sky,
That is how light.

The sound is like a hyena's joyful laugh.
They laugh through the day and laugh through the night,
That means they hardly sleep,
So in the morning they are not very bright!

It smells like gas,
It smells like laughing gas.

It tastes as though I'm drinking lime,
The sour, tingling, laughing lime.
It pops in your mouth, fizzing and crackling,
Maybe that's why I keep laughing when I drink it, all the time!

You get that funny feeling when it comes to you.
In the end, when you stop laughing,
You have a chance to say phew!

Zoe Ellison (9)
St Dominic's Catholic Junior School, Liverpool

Anger

Anger, to me, is extremely dark red,
I feel like no one cares about me.
Anger is horrible, it is like you're being
Forced to eat something you don't like.
It is even worse when someone is winding you up.

Anger is like Harry Potter getting hurt by Lord Voldemort.
When I am angry, it feels like there's
Steam coming out of my ears.
I get a flashback of something terrible,
I can smell burning, rotten eggs,
I feel like I want to attack the person
Who has made me angry.

Anger is like being in a dark room.

Karl Fleming (8)
St Dominic's Catholic Junior School, Liverpool

Fun

The colour of fun is orange like the sun.
I go wild like the other kids,
We act like fierce animals.

Fun tastes of delicious sweets and chocolate.
It's like a new Heaven.

It looks amazing, superb and brilliant,
Definitely hilarious and as bright as a button.

I feel my head filling up with happiness,
My heart beats with excitement.

I run around in circles screaming, 'Argh!'
It feels as great as green grass,
It's like a white blanket has been gently placed over everything.

It feels like chocolate melting in my mouth.
Fun smells of rich, juicy mango.

Fun reminds me of loud laughter and joy,
I open my mouth and shout, 'Ahh!'
The excitement is so much.
It reminds me of a flying pig.

My eyes widen.

Will Fleming (8)
St Dominic's Catholic Junior School, Liverpool

Fun

Fun is a feeling that tingles in my belly.
Fun is a word that is on the telly.
Blue is the world,
Pink is candyfloss,
Red is the funfair,
Silver is happiness,
Gold is laughter,
Yellow is a flower,
Orange is the feeling of butterflies in my tummy.
Fun means laughter.
Fun means happiness.

Lauren Grannell (8)
St Dominic's Catholic Junior School, Liverpool

Anger

Anger is like a roaring tiger.
Anger is like hailstones.
Anger is like very dark black.
Anger is like a rock.
Anger is a burning thing.

Anger is a taste of red-hot chilli peppers.
Anger is like smoke from a fierce fire.
Anger is a horrible thing.
Anger is the smell of rotten eggs.
Anger is a dark room.

Anger is like a flash of light.
Anger is a scary thing.
Anger is like a *thunderstorm!*

Jonathen Grey (8)
St Dominic's Catholic Junior School, Liverpool

Hate

The blood was squished, it was slithering down my throat.
I heard loud thunder
And I smelled the burning flesh of blood.
The taste was like blood water,
The colour was dark red,
It looked like blood soup
And it was really horrible.
It reminded me of horrible tomato soup.

Jamie Manning (8)
St Dominic's Catholic Junior School, Liverpool

Fear

You can tell fear because it smells like gas.
You can tell fear because it tastes like salty tears.
Fear is when you feel downhearted,
You feel it deep down inside,
You feel it deep down in the ground.

Fear is as scary as a ghost.
Fear is when you feel as small as a bouncy ball.
Fear is a land flowing away in the distance.
Fear is dark and gloomy.
Fear is the colour of indigo.
Fear is when you feel like you are on a deserted island.

Suzanne Ravenscroft (9)
St Dominic's Catholic Junior School, Liverpool

Darkness

Darkness, it makes me scared.
It is pitch-black,
It is disgusting,
It tastes like a tarantula is in my stomach.
It is horrible,
It smells like burning manure.
It is dark like coal in a small hole.
It is very solid,
It is very cold
And it is very bold,
And it comes from a fire.
It is that hot you would need gloves.
It is black all over,
It has got ash all over it
And it makes me sick.
It reminds me of fire.
I go red because it is horrible.

Deklan Richardson (9)
St Dominic's Catholic Junior School, Liverpool

Snowflakes Falling, Falling, Falling

I build a snowman
With crunchy, slippery snow.
I wrap a spotty scarf
Around his cold neck.
I put a warm hat
On his wet head.
I place some twigs
As his arms.
Next I place a carrot,
Then put olives for his buttons.
The twig arms put gloves on.
How long can my snowman last?

Maisie Harrison & Allan Fyles (7)
St Dominic's Catholic Junior School, Liverpool

Snow!

Snow, snow, snow,
How wonderful is snow?
Make snow angels and throw snowballs.
Snow, snow, snow,
I feel excited,
I feel delighted.

Megan Brady & Brooke McCoy (8)
St Dominic's Catholic Junior School, Liverpool

Snow, Snow

The day has come,
So we can play,
Go and play with
Our mate.

Fright, fright, fright,
The snow has come,
So we go out
To have some fun.

Playful, playful, playful,
Let's build a snowman,
Then throw snowballs
At each other.
But oh!
The snow keeps rising.

Caitlin Gilgannon (7) & Liam Phillips (8)
St Dominic's Catholic Junior School, Liverpool

Snow

Snow is white, it sparkles
Like a light coming down at night.
When it hits the ground
You cannot hear it,
But in the morning
It might stop snowing
And after breakfast,
I will let you go outside and play,
To say goodbye to the snow!

Jamie Horn (7) & Phoebe Dowling (8)
St Dominic's Catholic Junior School, Liverpool

What A Snowy Day!

Snow, snow, snow,
Have a snowball fight.
Snow, snow, snow,
It's been snowing all night.
Snow, snow, snow,
I feel excited.
Snow, snow, snow,
I also feel delighted.
Snow, snow, snow,
It's started to melt away.
Snow, snow, snow,
I will see you another day!

Leah Natteroy & Erin Johnston (8)
St Dominic's Catholic Junior School, Liverpool

Snow

White, white, white,
I got a fright,
Everywhere was white.

Crunch, crunch, crunch,
Underneath my feet,
Snow keeps on falling,
Dancing to the beat.

Fall, fall, fall,
Falling from the sky,
I can't seem to catch it,
No matter how I try!

Adam Carleton (7) & Stephen Sweeney (8)
St Dominic's Catholic Junior School, Liverpool

Snowing

The snow is fun,
The snow is cold,
It makes our fingers numb
And makes us fall on our bums!
The sky is grey,
The snow is white,
Oh what a wonderful,
Fantastic sight.

Taylor Owen (7) & Joanne Roberts (8)
St Dominic's Catholic Junior School, Liverpool

Snowing

Excited, excited, excited,
It had been snowing all night.
When I woke up,
It was a most fantastic sight.
I quickly got dressed
And ran outside.
Mum said, 'Hurry!
We'll go for a sledge ride.'

Anthony Ventre (8)
St Dominic's Catholic Junior School, Liverpool

Snow

It is a snowy day today,
We are happy.
Snowing, snowing, snowing,
We are playing in the snow.
We are having a lovely time
Till Mrs Cannon shouts, *'Wow!'*
And makes us slip on our bottoms.
It is fun, it is fine,
Snow is very bright,
I love snow.
Sparkly day, what a good day.
I make snow angels,
I have a snowball fight.
Now snow day is over,
I go to bed.

Nicole Hawksford (8)
St Dominic's Catholic Junior School, Liverpool

Snow

Snowing, snowing, snowing,
It has been snowing all night
And the snow is very bright.

Crunchy, crunchy, crunchy,
I make footprints in the snow
And all of a sudden, I have a frozen toe.

Drip, drip, drip,
The sun has come out to shine,
And this is the end of my sparkly time.

Rachel Gibbons (8)
St Dominic's Catholic Junior School, Liverpool

Summer

Summer is the best season in the year
And everyone can go out to the park
And to the swimming pool and you can
Go anywhere else.
I can go out for my birthday and
I can take my friends with me,
Or I can have a party and
I can invite my friends.
My sister comes with me wherever I go.
I go to the shops and my sister comes with me,
And my mum and nan come with me too.

Megan Daly (9)
St Dominic's Catholic Junior School, Liverpool

Love

Love is a feeling that tingles in my belly,
Love is a word that comes up on the telly.
Love is a crime that I think is ready,
Love is a thing that is rocking like 'hits melody'.

When I am in love I like to stare,
I like love because it is so sweet.
Love is kind,
Love is in my mind.

Lauren Sweeney (9)
St Dominic's Catholic Junior School, Liverpool

Love

Love is when you fall in love with someone.
Love is the colour of red.
Love tastes like sugar.
Love smells like it's on thin air.
Love looks so romantic,
It sounds so nice.
Love feels so lovely.

Courtney Foster (9)
St Dominic's Catholic Junior School, Liverpool

About My Family

I love my family
Because they are kind to me.
My family is special to me,
My family are all stars.
All my family buy me something every day.
I always do what I am told.
My family are wonderful.
All my family are Liverpool supporters, except two.
Liverpool is the best.
Steven Gerrard is one of my best players.
Liverpool are all my favourites.
I like my sisters.
My big sister buys me credit for my phone,
So do all my family,
They are really the best.

Charlie Shaw Johnson (9)
St Dominic's Catholic Junior School, Liverpool

Love

Love is a great thing,
Love is a thing,
Love is what you want,
Nearly everyone is in love.
Love is where you see someone,
Love is a big thing,
All parents have got love,
Children have got love as well.
I have got love.
When I see love,
It is just like a rose.

Louise Robinson (9)
St Dominic's Catholic Junior School, Liverpool

Tiny Toby

My dog Toby is not at all quiet,
To be quite honest, he can cause a riot,
But I love my dog, would you like to know why?
Because me makes me feel better when I'm having a cry.
When I tell him to go away,
He will not do that, he will just stay.
He turns my frown
Upside down.
Toby's real fast, we have a blast!
When he is asleep
I go in and have a peep.
When the ice cream van plays its song,
Toby will join in and sing along.
I love my Toby, he is great,
Come to think of it, he's my little mate.

Ellie Meskell (11)
St Dominic's Catholic Junior School, Liverpool

My Cat!

My cat Izzy is crazy.
She lies in front of the fire
On her red fluffy blanket.
My cat likes to lick her paws
And show everyone her long claws.
My cat is cool,
But acts like a fool.
She is great
And she's my little mate.
She chases her little ball,
So you have to give her a call.

Georgia Donnellan (11)
St Dominic's Catholic Junior School, Liverpool

One Cold Winter Morning

On this cold winter morning
The ground is as white as the top of a birthday cake.
I am deaf.
My ears ring as the cold air whispers down them.
Sugar cubes fall from the cloudy sky.
The white frozen ground reminds me of the fun I have.
Two big snowmen stand behind my shoulder, laughing.
Scoops of ice cream pass me at speed.
My laughter bellows through and out.
The funs stops when the bell rings.
School begins.

Ryan Horn (11)
St Dominic's Catholic Junior School, Liverpool

The Invisible Dog

Gazing across the misty park,
Memories of Tyson come flooding back.
In my mind's eye I see him,
His deep, soulful eyes almost appealing.
His floppy ears drooping down,
Hiding his eyes.
We ran around together
Like there was no end.
I remember the times we had together,
It seems like just yesterday.
Rolling in the mud for one last time.
Then I look back and he is gone.

Lauren Carleton (10)
St Dominic's Catholic Junior School, Liverpool

My Family!

My mum!
My mum is great,
She is my best mate.
My mum is so bubbly,
She is ever so cuddly.
My mum is mine
When she's had a glass of wine.

My dad!
My dad is cool,
He supports Liverpool.
My dad is footie mad,
He is the world's best dad.
My dad is no *fool,*
Plus he is never cruel.

My brother!
My brother is loud,
He is always proud.
My brother is funny,
He is my honey.
My brother is cool,
He is never a fool.

I love my family, they are the best,
Even though they're from the north west.
You can't have them, they're all mine,
It's a toast to them and a glass of wine.

Learna Manning (11)
St Dominic's Catholic Junior School, Liverpool

My Friend Ellie

My best friend is called Ellie
And she loves a lot of jelly.
My friend Ellie is so cool
And she is no stupid fool.
My friend Ellie is so cuddly
And she is so, so bubbly.
My friend Ellie is so funny
And she will always be my honey.

Rebecca Korbel (10)
St Dominic's Catholic Junior School, Liverpool

I Wish For Peace On Earth

Stop war, fighting, shooting and shouting,
Make love, friendship, peace and kindness.
I wish for love on Earth.
Stop drugs, alcohol, poverty and pollution,
Keep species protected.
I wish for peace on Earth.
Stop bullying, scaring, racism and swearing,
Make children safe, truthful and caring.
I wish for love on Earth.
Peace be with you.

Abbie Butterworth (11)
St Joseph's Catholic Primary School, Wallasey

Weakness

W eak is beating strong and changing people's souls.

E ating their strength is what weak is doing.

A nother day of terror capturing prisoners.

K indness has died, anger has risen.

N ever will we have freedom again.

E very day fear of death is killing me!

S tarvation has flown around the camp!

S eeing the deaths of so many people I wonder when is it my turn?

Daniel Berry (11)
St Joseph's Catholic Primary School, Wallasey

Misery Here

M isery haunts me!
I n the night worrying about my family
S cared - who's next for death to catch?
E xhaustion creeps around the camp
R oaring wind comes through the gaps in the walls
Y elling and arguing over old newspapers!

H unger stamps around grabbing us all!
E veryone is angry and just wants to escape!
R owing and shouting, cold and shivering!
E ndless pain runs through my body.

Becky Lavery (10)
St Joseph's Catholic Primary School, Wallasey

Freezing In Here

F reezing cold stabbing me
R avenous. I feel weak
E veryone screaming
E verything frozen, I'm going to die
Z apping the guards, I feel like doing
I n my dreams, darkness walks by
N azis invade every dream I have
G od is not helping me!

I f only we were fed and warm
N o hope of escape

H unger chasing me
E verything frozen, I'm going to die
R un? There's nowhere to go!
E veryone dying - I wonder if I'm next for the grave?

Jessica Hill (11)
St Joseph's Catholic Primary School, Wallasey

Hatred

H atred is running around

A nxious and weak, I can't move

T hinking of my family, what will happen to them?

R ooms are crowded, there's no more room

E veryone fights over newspapers

D oing nothing at all, just waiting for death!

Lois Kershaw (11)
St Joseph's Catholic Primary School, Wallasey

Prison

P ain creeps around the camp

R uined, my life is dead

I s there no escape from this camp?

S oon everyone will die

O ver the fence there is freedom!

N o one knows what is going to happen next!

Lauren Evans (10)
St Joseph's Catholic Primary School, Wallasey

Cold

C old smothers my skin
O n and off the light goes
L oneliness is slowly tearing me apart
D etermined to escape.

Niall Murphy (10)
St Joseph's Catholic Primary School, Wallasey

I Wish for . . .

Peace,
Everyone should get along together.
Peace,
Always for it to be safe in our homes and outside too.
Peace,
Clean water, no diseases, that is my wish.
Peace,
Every person should be treated the same as everyone else.

Eleanor Graham (11)
St Joseph's Catholic Primary School, Wallasey

Cold

Cold runs around us
Off and on the lights go
Cold runs around us.
Loneliness creeps up around us,
Cold runs around us.
Depression floats around us.
Cold runs around us.

Edward Cleary (10)
St Joseph's Catholic Primary School, Wallasey

Shalom

I wish for peace, not war.
I wish for people to be safe.
I wish for no bullying in the world.
I wish that all people were healthy.
I wish people looked after our planet.
I wish for no racism in the world.
I wish for joy and happiness and care.
Shalom.

James Cleary (10)
St Joseph's Catholic Primary School, Wallasey

Days

For one day and night,
Every day is another day.
You have money and homes,
The poor have none.
The poor live in sewers,
The poor are some of us.
We all need money and shelter,
Please give!

Nicholas Whittam (10)
St Joseph's Catholic Primary School, Wallasey

Giraffes

Giraffes are yellow with brown spots
And they mainly live in countries very hot

They have hooves on their feet
Which zookeepers keep neat.

They eat green leaves
From very tall trees.

My favourite animal is a giraffe,
I go to the zoo and they make me laugh.

They have four legs which run very quick
And a clever brain which makes them tick.

Melissa White (10)
St Joseph's Catholic Primary School, Wallasey

The Worst Literacy Lesson

The literacy lesson was over,
It was the most . . .
Eye-popping,
Ear-bursting,
Nail-biting,
Skin-crawling,
Spine-tingling,
Bone-chilling,
Blood-curdling
Two hours of my life.
I hate literacy.
Maybe I should not have become a poetry teacher.

Kelsey Caldwell (9)
St Joseph's Catholic Primary School, Wallasey

The Worst Book Of My Life

The book was over,
It was the most . . .
Skin-crawling,
Spine-tingling,
Eye-watering,
Spine-chilling,
Mouthwatering,
Mind-puzzling,
Bone-chilling,
Hair-raising,
Nail-biting,
Eye-popping,
Mind-boggling,
Ear-bursting,
Heartbreaking,
Gob-smacking
Experience of my life.
Guess what? I *loved* it!

Sinead Mooney (8)
St Joseph's Catholic Primary School, Wallasey

The Scary Film

The film was over,
It was the most . . .
Skin-crawling,
Blood-curdling,
Ear-bursting,
Spine-chilling,
Nail-biting,
Stomach-churning,
Bone-shaking,
Film of my life.
I really, really loved it.

Daisy Metcalfe (9)
St Joseph's Catholic Primary School, Wallasey

The Best Film

The film of the lion in the zoo was over,
It was the most . . .
Lip-smacking,
Nail-biting,
Hair-raising,
Ear-bursting,
Skin-crawling,
Spine-tickling,
Bone-chilling
Two hours of my life.
I want to be a lion
When I leave school.

Molly Lawton (8)
St Joseph's Catholic Primary School, Wallasey

The Football Game Was Over

It was the most . . .
Mind-puzzling,
Mouth-watering,
Heartbreaking,
Stomach-churning,
Nail-biting,
Mouth-watering,
Lip-smacking,
Heart-warming
Cup final ever.
And I scored the winning goal!
Come on!

Aiden Murray (8)
St Joseph's Catholic Primary School, Wallasey

My Worst Nightmare Ever

The nightmare was over,
It was the most . . .
Horrifying,
Blood-curdling,
Eye-popping,
Bone-chilling,
Nail-biting,
Spine-tingling,
Mind-numbing,
Hair-raising
Night of my life.
I loved it.

Mariah Clenkian (9)
St Joseph's Catholic Primary School, Wallasey

My Last Italian Meal

The meal was over,
It was the most . . .
Stomach-churning,
Skin-crawling,
Bone-chilling,
Hair-raising,
Nail-biting,
Lip-stinging,
Eye-popping,
Mind-blowing,
Blood-curdling
Italian meal of my life.
I loved it.

Kieron Jones (9)
St Joseph's Catholic Primary School, Wallasey

The Computer Game

The computer game was over,
It was . . .
Blood-curdling,
Spine-chilling,
Mind-puzzling,
Skin-crawling,
Eye-popping,
Stomach-churning,
Ear-splitting,
Spine-tingling,
Hair-raising,
It was the best thing in my life.

Georgia Croman (8)
St Joseph's Catholic Primary School, Wallasey

The Terrible Meal

My meal, it was the most . . .
Stomach-churning,
Blood-curdling,
Bone-chilling,
Lip-smacking,
Skin-crawling,
Eye-watering,
Hair-raising
Meal ever.
I hate Italian meals.

Matthew Harold (9)
St Joseph's Catholic Primary School, Wallasey

The Best Meal In The World

The meal was over,
It was the most . . .
Finger-licking,
Gob-smacking,
Mouthwatering,
Stomach-filling,
Lip-smacking
Hour of my life.
I never want it again.

Carl Whittam (8)
St Joseph's Catholic Primary School, Wallasey

The Great Italian Meal

The great Italian meal was over,
It was the most . . .
Mouth-watering,
Finger-licking,
Heart-warming,
Eye-watering,
Bone-chilling,
Mind-blowing,
Eye-popping,
Ear-bursting,
Lip-smacking,
Hair-raising,
Most horrible meal
In my life.

Molly Johnson (8)
St Joseph's Catholic Primary School, Wallasey

Derby Pool In New Brighton

The meal in the Derby Pool was over,
It was the most . . .
Mind-numbing,
Stomach-churning,
Nail-biting,
Mind-puzzling,
Eye-popping,
Eye-watering,
Ear-bursting,
Spine-chilling,
Mind-boggling
Experience of my life.
I love Spanish meals!

Jasmine Taylor-Sharp (8)
St Joseph's Catholic Primary School, Wallasey

The Terrible Holiday

The holiday was over,
It was the most . . .
Eye-popping,
Nail-biting,
Spine-chilling,
Eye-watering,
Mind-puzzling,
Blood-curdling
Week of my life.
I hate holidays.

James Orwin (9)
St Joseph's Catholic Primary School, Wallasey

Teddy Bears

Teddy bears are big,
Teddy bears are small,
It doesn't really matter
What they are at all.

They can be white,
They can be bright,
Or even red
And blue.

Some are ladies,
Some are babies
And some are men,
Of course.

Some wear ribbons,
Some wear ties,
But I know teddy bears
Will never die.

Paige Clayton (9)
St Joseph's Catholic Primary School, Wallasey

The Wraggle Taggle Singers

Three singers stood at the garden gate,
They sang so high, they sang so low;
The lady sat in her chair late,
Her heart it melted away as snow.

They sang so fast, they sang so shrill,
That fast her tears began to flow,
And she put down her electric bill,
TV control and all her show.

She took off her dressing gown,
Smiling happy down the stairs, O!
She walked in the street with smelly feet,
All out in the wind and weather, O!

'O, fetch my Ferrari
And go fetch a tuxedo, O!
That I may go and seek my bride,
Who is gone with the wraggle taggle singers, O!'

O he drove high and he drove low,
He swerved through wood and skidded too,
Until he came to
And there he saw his lady, O!

'What makes you leave your dressing gown?
Your Ferrari to forego?
What makes you leave your wedded man
To follow with the hippy vans, O!'

Ross Murray (10)
St Joseph's Catholic Primary School, Wallasey

Wildlife's Wacky Ways

One cheeky chimp chomping cheerfully,
Two pigeons pecking peacefully,
Three fat frogs flipping funnily,
Four friendly fish thinking friendly,
Five funny flamingoes fighting noisily,
Six stinky snakes swimming down the stream
Seven eager eels eating in England,
Eight growing giraffes grazing greedily,
Nine huge hippos having a holiday,
Ten green grasshoppers greedily gulping grapes.

Conor Lunn (10)
St Kentigern's RC Primary School, Blackpool

Untitled

One watery watermelon,
Two tangy toes,
Three amazing alligators,
Four flipping frogs,
Five funny fish,
Six slithery snakes,
Seven slow snails,
Eight gooey gates,
Nine wailing whales,
Ten hungry hippos.

Hayleigh Smith (9)
St Kentigern's RC Primary School, Blackpool

Alliteration Poem

One cuddly cat, Conker, catching cans,
Two bad bears bounce all the balls,
Three excited elephants eat eels,
Four dirty dogs dig deep down,
Five funny flies fly freely,
Six happy hippos all hope hard,
Seven giggling gorillas grow grapes,
Eight jumping jacks juggle for jets,
Nine kicking kids keep keys,
Ten lovely lions lick Liam.

Ben Campbell (9)
St Kentigern's RC Primary School, Blackpool

Animal Poem

One orange orang-utan,
Two tiny turtles,
Three little lines,
Four friendly fish,
Five foolish frogs,
Six silly suns,
Seven stupid snails,
Eight mad monkeys,
Nine nasty numbers,
Ten tangy tans.

Samantha Smith (9)
St Kentigern's RC Primary School, Blackpool

Number Poem

One wandering worm wiggled to Wales,
Two trendy tigers had long tails,
Three tangy toes eating mango,
Four flying fish drinking Tango,
Five funny frogs sitting on a leap pad,
Six stinky socks got very mad,
Seven shiny shoes sheltering from the rain,
Eight eating elephants are in pain,
Nine naughty knickers are nipping Neil,
Ten trusting turtles like eating orange peel.

Chelcee Starkie (10)
St Kentigern's RC Primary School, Blackpool

Terrible Tongue-Twisting Tales

One dizzy dog dozed on the doorstep,
Two terrible tortoises rumbled over the teapot,
Three naughty nits nibble on nice nuggets,
Four horrible horses hammered Henry's house,
Five fierce fish flying over Finland,
Six slimy snakes slither through Siberia,
Seven mad monkeys march up the mountain,
Eight lazy ladies lounge on a log,
Nine crazy cats crawl to the cradle,
Ten pretty penguins pecking at people.

Daisy Lonsdale (9)
St Kentigern's RC Primary School, Blackpool

Terrific Tongue Twisters

One crazy clown climbs out of a car,
Two lazy ladies look like llamas,
Three mischievous monkeys munch all the mangoes,
Four pretty peacocks peck at the peanuts,
Five raving rabbits run down the road,
Six slow sloths slumber sleepily,
Seven wiggly worms wiggle around the world,
Eight frisky frogs find four flies,
Nine dancing ducks do a difficult dance,
Ten heroic hens hop through the hailstones.

Joseph McMahon (10)
St Kentigern's RC Primary School, Blackpool

The Zoo

One chubby child chomping on chocolate,
Two mad monkeys munching on mangoes,
Three annoying alligators ambling,
Four flying fish fluttering in the air,
Five funny flies floating,
Six slithering snakes snarling,
Seven singing snails singing silently,
Eight eating elephants eating everything,
Nine tangy tomatoes tumbling,
Ten wandering werewolves wandering.

Anthony Platt (10)
St Kentigern's RC Primary School, Blackpool

Animal Control

One angry axeman ate ants,
Two bunnies bought bikes,
Three mad mice were mad monsters,
Four tough tigers taught the tortoise,
Five naughty nits nipped Nicholas,
Six chubby chimps chomped chocolate,
Seven excited elephants eat eels,
Eight funny flies fly forward,
Nine giggling gorillas growing grapes,
Ten dangerous dogs digging dirt.

Alex Houldsworth (10)
St Kentigern's RC Primary School, Blackpool

A Weird Poem

One noisy nail wailing on a wall,
Two red roosters rowing round a ring,
Three big balls bouncing like a baby,
Four fun frogs finding friends,
Five silly snakes slithering in sand,
Six sensible souls slipping on a slide,
Seven annoying ants fighting over an antler,
Eight intelligent igloos icing a cake,
Nine dangerous donkeys dangling on a door,
Ten tiling tigers tap-dancing on a table.

Aria Kiely (9)
St Kentigern's RC Primary School, Blackpool

World Cup!

(Based on 'Sheila's Wheels' song)

For the people who are football fans,
All across the nation's lands,
Yes you know we'll be victorious,
The atmosphere is glorious,
That's why we're number one!
Come on, let's have some fun!

As the ball rolls near the goal,
Along the pitch is Ashley Cole,
He tries to get the ball
To win it for us all,
But Ka Ka gets there first,
The crowd is gonna burst!

Goal, Goal,
Goal,
Goal,
Goal!

Emma O'Mahoney (10)
St Kentigern's RC Primary School, Blackpool

Chocolate!

I wish I had a chocolate bar
To go inside my belly,
To digest in my intestines,
While I am watching telly!

Galaxy is definitely the best,
The taste is just so scrummy,
But certainly by far and far,
It beats the sugar dummy!

Emma-Nicole Mansfield (9) & Katie O'Connell (10)
St Kentigern's RC Primary School, Blackpool

Granawocky

My gran's so sweet, she lives down the street,
I go to see her in my spare time.
When I do, she cooks a lovely stew,
She always greets me with a smile.

The cakes I love are the ones she cooks,
When I plead she always gives to me,
So I class her as the best granny.
Wherever I am, she is too.

I love her to bits, she'll be sadly missed,
She'll always be my angel grandma.
We'll meet again where she's gone to.
She is now in a safer place.

My gran's so sweet, she lives down the street,
I go to see her in my spare time.
When I plead, she gives to me.
When I go she makes a lovely stew,
She always greets me with a smile.

Aimee Morrissey-Hill (10)
St Kentigern's RC Primary School, Blackpool

The Magic Box

(Based on 'Magic Box' by Kit Wright)

I will put in the box . . .
A musical note played on a flute,
Blazes of flames from the sun,
A guitar with golden strings.

I will put in the box . . .
The last shining star before morning,
Thunder clattering on a stormy night,
The smell of smoke burning down a building.

I will put in the box . . .
A tiger with evil red eyes,
The sound of a truck engine roaring as if to explode,
And the claws of a jaguar.

I will put in the box . . .
A book that never ends,
The first step of a toddler
And the taste of lemon tingling on my tongue.

My box is fashioned from gold and jewels,
With lightning bolts on the lid, on a starry background.
Its hinges are made of razor-sharp teeth from a great white shark.

I shall play football in my box,
With crowds cheering crazily when I score.

Ivan Villarino (9)
St Kentigern's RC Primary School, Blackpool

What Is Orange?

Orange is the goose's beak
Pecking at its food.

Orange is the pumpkin
When it's Hallowe'en.

Orange is the sunset
Before I go to bed.

Orange is the fire
Burning on the hearth.

Orange is the baked beans
People like to eat.

Orange is the fruit,
Juicy in my mouth.

Orange is the marigolds
Growing in the meadow.

Orange is the carrot
Rabbits like to eat.

Katherine Foweather (8)
St Leonard's CE Primary School, Preston

What Is Green?

Green are the leaves
That grow on the tree.

Green is the grass
That I can see.

Green is the colour
Of my friend's eyes.

Green is the colour
Of my dad's ties.

Green is the paint
That we use in art.

Green is the signal
When we can start.

Green is the car
On my cousin's drive.

Green is the grasshopper
That's always alive.

Green is the colour
Of the bright, bright kite.

Green is the colour
That's always in sight.

Priya Manivannan (9)
St Leonard's CE Primary School, Preston

What Is Yellow?

Yellow is the colour of a healthy banana.
Yellow is the colour of an angel cake.
Yellow is as bright as a daffodil.
Yellow is the colour of an egg you use to bake.
Yellow is the bright sun.
Yellow is like the bright yellow stars.
Yellow is a lemon, bitter and sour.
Yellow is the colour of a sweet fluffy duck.

Rebecca Jack (9)
St Leonard's CE Primary School, Preston

Yellow

Yellow is the sun.
Yellow are the buttercups shining.
Yellow is the butter glowing.
Yellow are the daffodils growing.
Yellow are the lemons.
Yellow are the bananas hanging off a tree.
Yellow is the sweetcorn.

Danyelle Hodgson (9)
St Leonard's CE Primary School, Preston

Summer

Summer comes
With birds singing.

Summer comes
With swimming pools flowing.

Summer comes
With the sun blazing.

Summer comes
With bees stinging.

Summer comes
With cows chewing.

Summer comes
With ducks swimming.

Summer comes
With children playing.

Summer comes
With ice creams melting.

Ben Hargreves (9)
St Leonard's CE Primary School, Preston

Happiness

Happiness tastes like ice cream.
Happiness is the colour green.
Happiness sounds like laughs.
Happiness looks like a big bowl of ice cream.
Happiness reminds me of my family.
Happiness feels like chocolate.
Happiness smells like roses.

Rhys Massaro (8)
St Leonard's CE Primary School, Preston

Spring

Spring comes
With egg rolling.

Spring comes
With chicks hatching.

Spring comes
With lambs leaping.

Spring comes
With rivers flowing.

Spring comes
With grass growing.

Spring comes
With sun lasting.

Spring comes
With trees budding.

Spring comes
With flowers growing.

Alex Calderbank (8)
St Leonard's CE Primary School, Preston

Blue

Blue is the sunny sky soaring above.
Blue are the blue tits flying in the wind.
Blue are the bluebells giving their scent.
Blue is the school jumper at my school.
Blue is the ocean thrashing its waves.
Blue are the blue whales swimming in the sea.
Blue are the blueberries sitting on a bush.

Daniel Lawler (8)
St Leonard's CE Primary School, Preston

Summer Comes

Summer comes
With the sun shining.

Summer comes
With children playing.

Summer comes
With flowers growing.

Summer comes
With birds singing.

Summer comes
With rivers flowing.

Summer comes
With planes flying.

Summer comes
With babies shouting.

Summer comes
With people eating.

James Robinson (9)
St Leonard's CE Primary School, Preston

Anger

Anger is the colour of red.
Anger tastes like blood and sweat.
Anger looks dark and red.
Anger smells like mud.
Anger sounds like screaming and rowing.
Anger reminds me of *fire*.
Anger feels like being hurt.

Oliver Cuerden (9)
St Leonard's CE Primary School, Preston

Winter

Winter comes
With flowers dying.

Winter comes
With animals hibernating.

Winter comes
With rain dropping.

Winter comes
With wind blowing.

Winter comes
With ground freezing.

Winter comes
With snow falling.

Winter comes
With people shivering.

Winter comes
With Christmas coming.

Bradley Reid (9)
St Leonard's CE Primary School, Preston

Winter

Winter comes
With ice coming.

Winter comes
With snow falling.

Winter comes
With the doorbell jamming.

Winter comes
With the sky dulling.

Winter comes
With rain dropping.

Winter comes
With wet playtimes approaching.

Karl Riley (9)
St Leonard's CE Primary School, Preston

Pink

Pink is the colour of lipstick
Shining on the ladies' lips.

Pink is the colour of nail varnish
Glowing on fingertips.

Pink is the colour of dresses,
Dancing to the music.

Pink is the colour of the beautiful shoes
Sparkling on the dance floor.

Pink is the colour of handbags
That ladies use for shopping.

Pink is the colour of hair slides
That stop ladies hair from dropping.

Pink is the colour of roses,
With lovely smells for noses.

Genavieve Borg (9)
St Leonard's CE Primary School, Preston

Summer Comes

Summer comes
With sun shining.

Summer comes
With sweat dripping.

Summer comes
With birds singing.

Summer comes
With children shouting.

Summer comes
With balls flying.

Summer comes
With people playing.

Summer comes
With people drinking.

Summer comes
With waves roaring.

Matthew Davis (9)
St Leonard's CE Primary School, Preston

What Is Blue?

Blue is the sky
In spring when it's sunny.

Blue is the sea
Roaring at the wind.

Blue are the jeans
That we wear on holiday.

Blue are the bluebells
That grow in the summer.

Blue are the dolphins
Swimming in the sea.

Blue is our school uniform
That we wear at school.

Blue are our lips
When they get cold in the winter.

Asha Nayli (9)
St Leonard's CE Primary School, Preston

What Is Yellow?

Yellow is the sun
That shines in the sky.

Yellow is the syrup
That drips from the spoon.

Yellow are the lemons
That grow on the tree.

Yellow is the honey
That the bees have made.

Yellow are the buttercups' petals
That shimmer in the sun.

Yellow is the butter
I put on my toast.

Yellow is the colour
I love the most.

Clara Butler (8)
St Leonard's CE Primary School, Preston

Summer Comes

Summer comes
With plants growing.

Summer comes
With birds tweeting.

Summer comes
With children shouting.

Summer comes
With a sprinkler spraying.

Summer comes
With presents arriving.

Summer comes
With decorations flying.

Luke Wilson (8)
St Leonard's CE Primary School, Preston

What Is Blue?

Blue is the sea,
And also a swimming pool.

Blue is the uniform
That we wear to school.

Blue is the sky
Where planes fly high.

Blue are the berries
That make a delicious pie.

Blue are the birds
That fly high in the sky.

Blue are the bluebells
That grow very high.

Emily Brown (8)
St Leonard's CE Primary School, Preston

What Is Blue?

Blue is the colour
Of your nose.

Blue is the colour
Of my toes.

Blue is the colour
Of your tie.

Blue is the colour
Of my eyes.

Blue is the colour
Of your car.

Blue is the colour
Of my jar.

Blue is the colour
Of your boat.

Blue is the colour
Of my coat.

Phoebe Child (8)
St Leonard's CE Primary School, Preston

Sadness

Sadness comes
With friends arguing.

Sadness comes
With tastes of blood.

Sadness comes
With people crying.

Sadness comes
With no friends.

Sadness comes
With the smell of friends.

Sadness comes
With cloudy black skies.

Harriet Devine (8)
St Leonard's CE Primary School, Preston

What Is Pink?

Pink is the colour of a bright rose.
Pink is the colour of a floating balloon.
Pink is the colour of an underwater hippo.
Pink is the colour of a tall tulip.
Pink is the colour of a farmyard pig.
Pink is the colour of a one-legged flamingo.
Pink is the colour of a smelly lipstick.
Pink is the colour of an evening dress.
Pink is the colour of a strawberry bubblegum sweet.

Harriet Smith (8)
St Leonard's CE Primary School, Preston

What Is Yellow?

Yellow is the colour of
The sun that shines so bright.

Yellow is the colour of
A tiger ready to fight.

Yellow is the colour of
A light bulb when it's on and has power.

Yellow is the colour of
Your hair when it's been conditioned in the shower.

Yellow is the colour of
A plant pot standing still on the ground.

Yellow is the colour of
Telephones making a *ring, ring* sound.

Yellow is the colour of
Bananas, ripe and ready to eat.

Yellow is the colour of
Cloudy lemonade, so sugary and sweet.

Yellow is the colour of
Candle wax slowly melting.

Yellow is the colour of
A lion loudly yelping.

Yellow is the colour of
Daffodils rising up in spring.

Yellow is the colour of
White wine that makes people sing.

Yellow is the colour of
Wood that is called beech.

Yellow is the colour of
Sand that is on a beach.

Emma Kulbacki (9)
St Leonard's CE Primary School, Preston

Sadness

Sadness feels like tears and rain.
Sadness sounds like crying.
Sadness is blue like ice.
Sadness tastes like salty sweat.
Sadness reminds me of sleep.
Sadness looks like loneliness.
Sadness smells like air.

Alex Sahillioglu (9)
St Leonard's CE Primary School, Preston

Spring

Spring comes
With leaves growing.

Spring comes
With flowers opening.

Spring comes
With ducks being born.

Spring comes
With lambs skipping.

Spring comes
With warmer weather.

Spring comes
With sun appearing.

Spring comes
Once a year.

Spring comes
With new shoots.

Niall Riley (8)
St Leonard's CE Primary School, Preston

Spring Comes

Spring comes
With cocoons opening.

Spring comes
With butterflies flying.

Spring comes
With rain stopping.

Spring comes
With flowers growing.

Spring comes
With mud drying.

Thomas Hampson (9)
St Leonard's CE Primary School, Preston

What Is Yellow?

Yellow is the sun that shines in the sky.
Yellow is the lolly that people have as they go by.
Yellow is the sand that lays on the beach.
Yellow is the buttercup that lays on the land.
Yellow is the butter that's spread on toast.
Yellow is the raincoat that stops you from getting wet.

Shelby Preston (8)
St Leonard's CE Primary School, Preston

A Spooky Spell In Shakespeare's Style

In my spell, so spooky for a crime,
I will put in these ingredients of mine:

Foot of girl and ear of boy,
Electrifying part of toy,
Slime of toad, nose of dog,
Toe of tiger, voice box of frog,
Heart of rat and dragon's scale,
Feathers of owl, skin of whale,
Head of cobra, tail of mouse,
Root of grass from under a house.
'Double, double, toil and trouble,
Fire burn and cauldron bubble.'

Jenny Parker (10)
St Paul's RC Primary School, Blackburn

Remembrance

After the dreadful war,
The brave army dying
On the grassy field,
Gleaming poppies sprout
Where soldiers lost their lives.
Lonely widows cry.
The screaming battle ends.
Generous Tom Lister helps
Poor war veterans have homes.

Howard Livesey (10)
St Paul's RC Primary School, Blackburn

Football

Our football team's the best,
We always beat the rest.
We always win, we never lose,
But we sometimes blow a fuse.
Our football team's the best,
We always beat the rest.
We sometimes kick the ball too hard
And it lands in a bird's nest.

Adam Burgess (10)
St Paul's RC Primary School, Blackburn

Macbeth

Crocodile teeth ripped from jaw,
Crushed rat from my door,
Lizard skin, dry and hard,
Cobra teeth, milked and jarred.
Voles' bones pulled from owl guts,
Hunter eyes and tongues from mutts.
Devil horns, hollow scraped
And a mummy's head that's been taped.
'Double, double, toil and trouble,
Fire burn and cauldron bubble.'

Ben O'Ryan (11)
St Paul's RC Primary School, Blackburn

The Built Environment

Diagonal, dark, spaced bricks,
A gleeful red door
A bumpy slate roof,
Which sits in the heat
Smiling out brightly,
Glowing its cherry-red bricks!

Bright, dark, pale and dull,
White, black, grey, cream,
The bricks are all different,
A spectacular variety on display,
With texture smooth,
Matching the sky
As the sun goes down!

James Jackson (10)
St Paul's RC Primary School, Blackburn

For Your Tomorrow, I Gave My Today

For your tomorrow, I gave my today.
I wandered around like a stray cat at night,
I didn't want to, but I had to fight.
For your tomorrow, I gave my today.

The poppies stood up brave and proud,
The poppies saluted me night and day.
The poppies bent down to where I lay.
The poppies stood up brave and proud.

I gave my life for your salvation.
The soldiers' wounds cried out with blood.
The soldiers lay down in the mud.
I gave my life for your salvation.

For your tomorrow, I gave my today.

Chloe McGrath (10)
St Paul's RC Primary School, Blackburn

A Poem For Remembrance

If my son hadn't gone to war,
He'd still be here with me.
He would have been married by now,
If he hadn't gone to war.

Maybe I wanted him to go,
It was his dream, his life.
I only wanted my son to be an escort for me
When I was old and when I died, and he would
If he hadn't gone to war.

I loved him with my heart,
He was all I had left.
He would have been back by now
If he hadn't gone to war.

He's buried in a German graveyard,
I've only been to see him once, they hardly let me in.
He should be with me if anything,
If my son hadn't gone to war.

For our tomorrow, he gave his today.

Jenna Parkinson (11)
St Paul's RC Primary School, Blackburn

Remembrance

Remember the soldiers
Who fought in the war,
Just thinking of them
Makes us feel sorrow.

Remember those who fought
And died ever so terribly.
The muddy poppy fields
Embraced the soldiers lovingly.

Remember all the widows
Who lived life outside solemnly,
The workhouses cried out
To the single widows hungrily.

Remember the families
At the war's end they did mourn.
Distress took over,
All the families forlorn.

Eleanor Rawstron (11)
St Paul's RC Primary School, Blackburn

Remembrance

We thank you every day
For the words that you say,
Because you went to fight,
My house is not alight.
You helped us cope,
Through love and hope.
We do not like the war,
It makes us feel poor.
The loved ones we lost,
Nothing can ever repay the cost.

Charlotte McManus (10)
St Paul's RC Primary School, Blackburn

Perfect Poison

Smooth dragon's scale,
Long rat's tail,
Hairy pink monkey's arm,
Sharp, spiky tree palm,
Multicoloured rhino's horn,
Fresh tigers born,
Piles of leopard's skin,
Dirt from last week's bin,
Big bats' huts,
Cold sharks' guts,
Fat slugs' slime,
Pigeons' grime.
Bubble, bubble, burn and boil,
Solution freeze and pour in soil.

Anna Moorman (10)
St Paul's RC Primary School, Blackburn

The Day At The Zoo

The monkey swinging,
The elephant spraying,
The lions roaring,
The birds squawking.

The penguins sliding,
The rhino barging,
The gorillas are shouting, 'Ooh-ooh, ah-ah!'
The giraffe is as tall as a tree.

As I was walking to the café
A gorilla went, 'Ooh-ooh, ah-ah!'
And escaped!

Alex Tudge (8)
St Peter's CE Primary School, Bolton

Before The Storm

Black skies,
Scare me.
Icy rain
Wets me.
Run quickly,
Guide me.
Home safe,
Lead me.
As the thunder roars
Help me,
Save me,
Support me,
Get me home.

William Lee (8)
St Peter's CE Primary School, Bolton

Being Deaf

I have never heard the birds sing,
Although I have seen them flap their wings.
I have never heard the children play,
But I always see the break of day.
I have never heard a kettle whistle,
But I have seen a purple thistle.
I have never heard a church bell ring,
But I have watched the choir sing.
I have never heard a trumpet toot,
But I have seen a pair of boots.
I have never heard the April showers,
But love to look at springtime flowers.
Being deaf can be lonely,
I wish I could hear . . . if only.

Rebecca Townsend (9)
St Peter's CE Primary School, Bolton

The Big Match

Big match,
Encourage me,
So we win,
Guide me.
Football manager shouts at me,
Soccer, kids so care,
Tempt me,
Football mates tell me,
Lead me,
Parents love me,
Cheer me on,
Support me,
I could run all match.
My heart is cheering,
My heart is pumping,
Help me.
Drink a lot,
Find me,
Full-time,
Reward me.

Matthew Wills (8)
St Peter's CE Primary School, Bolton

My Best Friend

My best friend is great,
She is a girl
And my best mate.

We have our ups and downs.
Sometimes we have sleepovers
With our dressing gowns.

We get along quite nicely,
I suppose she's the clever one,
Mmm, precisely.

I go round to her house,
She comes round to mine.
I think we both agree,
We'll be friends 'til the end of time.

Georgina Kilmartin (9)
St Peter's CE Primary School, Bolton

About My Cousin, Dana

Dana is really close to me,
She is as sweet as sweets,
I love her to bits.

We have things in common,
Like we eat peas for our tea,
Brush our hair like fleas.

She is six years old,
Like my butty growing mould.
She likes to draw my mum crawling.

Kirsty Green (10)
St Peter's CE Primary School, Bolton

My Brother

My brother is a cool dude,
But he walks round in the nude.
My mum gets in a bad mood
And says, *'That's rude!'*

My brother is always dirty,
He has a bear called Bertie.
His girlfriends are flirty.

My brother is loud
And he is proud.
His favourite word is crowd.

I love my brother,
I'm like his mother.
I'm glad we get on with each other!

Amy Tudge (10)
St Peter's CE Primary School, Bolton

Before The Show

Help me,
Guide me,
Make me funny.
Support me,
Cheer me on,
Think I am funny,
Laugh with me,
Not at me.
Try not to get booed,
Make people laugh,
Encourage me.

Abigail Cooper (9)
St Peter's CE Primary School, Bolton

Before The School Test

Clever teacher,
Train me.
Best friends,
Encourage me.
Loving mum and dad,
Help me.
Helpful family
Support me.
God help me get high scores.
As the tables are pulled away,
So may I do my best.
As the children go quiet,
I will do my best.

Molly Fitton (9)
St Peter's CE Primary School, Bolton

Good Luck To My Milly

Numeracy
Helps me.
Teachers
Teach me.
Guide me to my times tables.
My mum
Guides me.
My friends
Support me.
My dad
Leads me.
Good luck to my times tables.

Jessica Wonta (8)
St Peter's CE Primary School, Bolton

Training Begins

Train me,
Hard work.
Help me,
Aching arms.
Support me,
Cheering,
Tempt me
Towards my opponent.
While adrenaline's pumping,
The sweat trickles down,
So may I
Avoid the opponent
Of my fellow boxers.

Joe Madden (9)
St Peter's CE Primary School, Bolton

Before The Swimming Championship

Help me with my bobbing,
Stop my leg from throbbing.
Don't let me sink, is what I
Don't want to think.
Let the water be clean,
Help the people not to be mean.
Let the teacher guide me,
Help the people beside me.
Let the walls be steady,
Help me to be ready.
Help me round the gaps that are tiny,
Let the weather be shiny.
Be my guard,
Train me hard,
Help me to float to the top.
Don't let the baby's rubber ring pop.
Help me to be fast,
Don't let people in with a cast.

Teejay Jackson (8)
St Peter's CE Primary School, Bolton

My First Day At School

I was feeling very nervous
On my first day at school.
All the people there
Made me look like a fool.

I was feeling very happy
When I met my first teacher.
I was feeling very happy
When I met all my friends.

All my friends there
Made me feel very happy.

Rebecca Larkin (9)
St Peter's CE Primary School, Bolton

Colours

Blue is like the sea,
Red is like a rose,
Green is like the shiny grass,
Yellow is like a pyramid,
Gold is like a goldfish,
Black is like the night sky,
White is like a piece of paper.

Orange is like some paint,
Grey is like some hair,
Brown is like some pants,
Pink is like a raspberry,
Purple is like a top,
Violet is like a book.

Daniel Brabin (9)
St Peter's CE Primary School, Bolton

Colours

Baby-blue is as blue as the sky,
Red is as juicy as an apple,
Brown is a tree trunk,
I am as red as lips.
Yellow is as bright as the sun,
White is as white as a feather.
All the colours round the world.

Green is like a leaf,
Pink is like our faces,
Black is like midnight,
Grey is like the moon,
Purple is like the sky.

Courtney Jackson (8)
St Peter's CE Primary School, Bolton

Before The Show

Lead me,
Guide me,
Help me to do my best.

Make me strong,
Help me win,
Love me
When I do my show.

Kai Belk (8)
St Peter's CE Primary School, Bolton

Before The Swimming Award

Before the swimming award,
Loving parents
Encourage me,
My team
Help me,
All my family
Support me,
My friends
Guide me
Towards my gold awards.

As my legs kick the water,
Everyone watches.
I avoid the slippery floor
Near the swimming pool.
I wear armbands
And they stick to my arms.

So may I
Not be tired.
Splendid trainers award me.
Happy parents cheer me.
Help me get all my awards.

Bethany Greenhalgh (9)
St Peter's CE Primary School, Bolton

A Day At The zoo

A gorilla gobbled the banana,
The snake slithered across the floor, all scaly and rough.
Everyone saw the green crocodile,
It roared as loud as the thunderstorm.

Everyone was happy as the squirrels took seed off them.
The dolphin jumped right up to the sky.
When it came back, it splashed everyone
From head to toe.

The elephant drank water then washed itself.
The monkey swung from tree to tree,
Searching for a banana to eat.

Rachel Wolstencroft (9)
St Peter's CE Primary School, Bolton

Before The Singing Award

Silver microphone,
Guide me.
All my family
Encourage me.
Music signs
Find me.
Singing teacher,
Support me.
My friends
Push me
To winning the award
As everyone cheers my name.
I know I've got to win
So may I
Avoid being booed
By other parents,
As I sing my last line
I think I'm gonna win,
So may I get the award.
My splendid voice helps me,
Excited parents cheer me.
Let me win the award!

Aaliyah Westhead (9)
St Peter's CE Primary School, Bolton

Emotion

E is for excitement
M oving in my heart
O verwhelming feelings
T apping at every part
I ncredible it might seem
O ozing from the start
N othing can explain the emotion from my heart.

Katie Mullings (8)
Stamford Park Junior School, Altrincham

Laughter

At the park I shut my eyes,
I hear laughter,
I feel happy, I want to skip, run, somersault,
The best I've ever done!

I feel light, free, a tiger who's just escaped from the zoo.
I smell summer flowers and freshly cut grass.
I taste cool summer breeze, as cold as ice cream.
I taste lemon tart just come from the oven.

I hear blue birds singing a heavenly choir,
Pixies dancing, skipping, jumping,
Lion roaring, donkeys braying.
I see yellow sun, flowers blooming,
Lakes with fish of many colours.

I feel happy.
I open my eyes and laugh along.

Anna Cooper (8)
Stamford Park Junior School, Altrincham

Fun

Fun is exciting in some way that makes you want to play
But when you play, you just want to say hooray.
When the rain starts to pour
You will need to go home to your drawers
And pull out your slippers and put them on.
When you are done, go and have some fun,
Not out, just in,
And the fun will begin.
But after 3 o'clock you will have to go down for tea.
After tea you will need a toffee or a coffee,
And after, you go to bed instead.

Chanelle Burke Robinson (7)
Stamford Park Junior School, Altrincham

Love

There are lots of things that I love
That have been sent from God up above,
Like sweets, chocolate and vanilla ice cream.
All different colours - red, pink and green.

I love my Heelies, my skates and skipping rope too.
I love to ski in France on runs that are blue.
But most of all I love my mum, dad and brother, Tom.
The thunder in my heart feels like a bomb.

They all make me laugh, they make me giggle as well,
The feeling in my heart just makes me wiggle, I must tell.
This poem is for them, I want them to know,
I just want to kiss them, then wrap them in a bright red bow.

Louise Scotson (8)
Stamford Park Junior School, Altrincham

Emotions

Anger is very bitter, it's glowing bright red.
Anger is a drum pounding deep inside my head.

Happy is kind, happy is my friend,
Happy is so kind his friendship just won't end.

When you are not happy you tend to get sad,
When you get sad it's always something bad.

Fear can be scary,
Like a troll that's big and hairy.

I'd think of a dove
As a symbol of love.

Philip Owen (7)
Stamford Park Junior School, Altrincham

How I Feel

When I'm feeling happy, a smile's upon my face,
But when there is a frown, tears roll down my cheek.
So when I am bright red I am full of anger.
Then when I turn bright green, I think I'm going to be sick.
Bleugh!

Amy Mather (7)
Stamford Park Junior School, Altrincham

The Sea

The sea is blue with white waves,
It crashes against the rocks making a shushing sound.
When the wind blows, the sea becomes
Angry, crazy and mad.

But when the sea is calm and gentle, it is still and clear
And you can swim and paddle.
When the sea is peaceful, it looks
Like a big, bright blue carpet.

If you taste the salty sea,
It will make you shiver and quiver.
But I like going to the sea because
It reminds me of happiness and laughter with my family.

Mollie Axon (8)
Stamford Park Junior School, Altrincham

Love

My heart is full of love,
As if to love everyone.
Love your family as you love yourself.
Love is happiness, laughter and fun.
Love everyone in the world.
Love your school; love your teacher and your friends.
Love is what life should be.

Katy Cai (8)
Stamford Park Junior School, Altrincham

What Is Fun?

Fun is the colour orange,
Juicy oranges, new and fresh,
Golden sunshine on a hot summer's day,
Glowing Spanish sunset.

Fun is the taste of candyfloss melting on my tongue,
Cheese and pineapple on sticks,
Chocolate cake with Smarties on.

Fun is sliding, bouncing, jumping, skipping and chasing,
Climbing tall trees, swinging like monkeys.

Fun is the sound of giggling in the park,
The whistle of bamboo waving in the wind,
The blowing out of birthday candles.

Fun is a tickly cuddle, the wind on my cheeks,
A bouncy castle that is my bed,
A warm duvet at the end of a busy day
With a cosy teddy and a night-time kiss.

Rosie Peachey (7)
Stamford Park Junior School, Altrincham

My Emotion Inventions

My little love dove
My laughter crafter
My little dark spark
My little fear deer
My hunger tunger
My little fun bun
My anger banger
My little hate bait
My sadness addness.

Sadie Tully (9)
Stamford Park Junior School, Altrincham

My Honest Feelings

When I feel happy
I put a smile across my face.
When I feel sad,
I want to be in another place.
When I feel loved,
I want to hug my family inside.
When I feel hungry,
I want to eat food inside
Like waves crashing over a tide.

Emma Davies (9)
Stamford Park Junior School, Altrincham

What Is Sadness?

If sadness were a colour, it would be grey.
Grey is a dark, dull and unhappy colour.
Grey is the colour of dark clouds and rain.

When I'm sad, the sound I make is crying.
The sound of the rain makes me feel worse.
When you're sad it's hard to think.

The taste of sadness is like eating a worm,
A horrible taste that you can never forget.

Instead of bouncing, jumping and skipping,
When you're sad you walk around in the rain
Or lie in your bed and can't get to sleep.

Sadness reminds me of sharp thorns.

Lottie Peachey (9)
Stamford Park Junior School, Altrincham

Sounds Of Feelings

The sound of sadness, sobbing, sobbing at a loss.
The sound of anger, burning, burning until it goes black.
The sound of fear, a machine gun firing in your head.
The sound of love, doves fluttering in the air.
The sound of hate, screams and shouts.
The sound of hunger, tummies rumbling.
The sound of jealously, a light wind getting stronger and stronger.
The sound of laughter, the hyenas in 'The Lion King'.
The sound of loneliness, your own heart beating.
The sound of tiredness, your head sinking down into your pillow.

Helen Cohen (9)
Stamford Park Junior School, Altrincham

Friendship

F riendship,
R emember them,
I magine it,
E normous friendship,
N ever forget them,
D ash to them,
S hare with them.

Chloe Knowles (9)
Stamford Park Junior School, Altrincham

Happiness

Happiness is like going to Wales,
You feel relaxed looking up at the stars,
All so proud when we get Mars bars,
Having barbecues just at the tent,
Fetching water (always sent),
You enjoy meeting people and forever playing,
Listening to what everyone's saying.

I always enjoy playing with my dog,
But not when her ball gets lost in the fog.
When we have dinner we all feel great,
We all love it when we go to bed late.
When we go to the sea we always play,
Right to the dawn of day.
When it's nice we fly a kite,
Then we're all back at the site.
We normally laugh at going crabbing,
Even when the sea is ebbing.

We play on mountains made of sand,
Most of them cover the land.
We take the dogs out five times each day,
Though they never tell us when they want to play.

Julia Madeley (9)
Stamford Park Junior School, Altrincham

Happiness

Things that I think of when I'm happy:

Church bells ringing,
Doves flying in the sky,
Bright colours like yellow and orange,
My best, fantastic friends,
My caring, loving family,
A choir singing, 'O Come All Ye Faithful',

I think of these things when I'm happy, like now.

Euan Gilchrist (8)
Stamford Park Junior School, Altrincham

Bullied

I'm very sad, too sad in fact,
And soon it will turn into anger,
But I'm not being bad.

Getting bullied each week, each day,
I can't believe how it's made me feel.
So scared, so nervous, so worried.
I believe it's very wrong.
What am I to do?

Ava Mullen-Cooper (9)
Stamford Park Junior School, Altrincham

Animals

Animals can be used as pets,
Animals can go to vets.

Dogs can go and fetch a bone,
Cats can whine, miaow and moan.

Ponies can eat and sleep,
Parrots you can sometimes keep.

Bears are scary and have sharp teeth,
Cows are boring but give nice beef.

Rabbits always get told
They always have to be as good as gold.

Pigs are always fat, not thin,
Some can be the size of a bin.

Sheep are very fluffy to make wool,
They are not nearly as big as a bull.

Birds are made to fly,
How can they, 'cause they have tiny eyes?

Allicia Birch (8)
Stamford Park Junior School, Altrincham

The Emotional Rainbow

Red is anger, full of rage makes me mad.
Orange is excitement, lively, bouncy, bubbly and glad.
Yellow is happiness, being sunny makes me bright,
.Green is peace, chilled, relaxed, everything's right.
Blue is sad, down in the dumps, feeling low.
This colour is magical, mysterious, *indigo*.
Violet is proud, let your feelings show.
Here are the colours of the emotional rainbow.

Molly Harrison (9)
Stamford Park Junior School, Altrincham

Seasonal Feelings

Winter brings you fun and laughter,
With Christmas and New Year.
The season remembered forever after
And the parties give us cheer.

Spring brings you happiness and love,
With lambs and chicks all round.
The birds are flying up above
And flowers are on the ground.

Summer brings you peace and joy,
With sunbathing on the beach.
The children are playing, girls and boys,
And no need for teachers to teach.

Autumn brings you all these things,
With leaves all falling down.
The laughter just makes you want to sing
And the love takes away your frown.

Ruth Owen (9)
Stamford Park Junior School, Altrincham

Fun

Fun is a pleasure
Fun is a game
Fun never ever measures the pain
Fun is laughter
Fun is sweet
When hearts like people meet
Fun is soft
Fun is happy
When crocodiles are very snappy
Fun is nice
Fun is play
When you're having fun by the bay
Fun is furry
Fun is jolly
While eating a strawberry lolly
Fun is velvet
Fun is smooth
While having fun in youth
Fun is sugar
Fun is spice
When lots of people are very nice
Fun is cool
Fun is fun
When the chores have been done.

Tom Stenning (10)
Stamford Park Junior School, Altrincham

The Star Of Hope

Darkness gushing into the hearts of the innocent,
Sending only the dread of hate,
Suddenly a blinding white light seeps
Through cracks in the atmosphere,
A multitude of glinting stars,
A glistening,
A glowing,
Wash away the fear,
Though darkness is around us,
Hope is always near.

Aoife Gilchrist (10)
Stamford Park Junior School, Altrincham

Happiness

Happiness is like a soft, cuddly teddy,
A crowd of children laughing and playing,
The smell of perfume wafting around,
With the shining sun spreading the world with happiness.

Happiness is like fluffy cats sitting on a wall,
A Heaven on Earth,
The taste of sugar and ice cream
With the merriment of Christmas.

Happiness is like a colourful rainbow,
A velvety rug,
The sound of giggling
With the bliss of a summer holiday.

Daisy Stacey (10)
Stamford Park Junior School, Altrincham

Emotion

Love is a lake that is crystal clear,
Fear is the moon casting a frightful leer.

Hope is a light shining out from the dark,
Hate is a blindfold, riddled with marks.

Joy is the stars, right up in front,
Rage is a bull with a roaring grunt.

Desire is a blanket that is warm and soft
And guilt is a dagger that stabbed you aloft.

Robert Adams (9)
Stamford Park Junior School, Altrincham

Hunger

When I feel hunger,
I think of all my favourite foods.
I think of ice, cold, cold,
On a red-hot beach,
But when I'm cold
I think of hot chocolate with
Pink and white marshmallows on top.
But one of my favourite foods
Is the red-hot chilli.

Conor Cooke (10)
Stamford Park Junior School, Altrincham

Hunger

I see all of those juicy jelly beans with different
flavours. I touch pizza boxes like wooden
blocks. It smells like melted mozzarella.
I hear the sizzle of crispy bacon in
an oily pan sizzling like fire. I
smell chips from the fish and
chip shop frying away
in a greasy fryer like
a growling tiger.
I feel hungry
for an ice
cream.
Time
for
tea,
OK?

Huw Jenkins (10)
Stamford Park Junior School, Altrincham

Anger!

Anger is like spicy, hot curry.
Anger feels like a flaming hot volcano about to erupt.
Anger tastes like burnt toast.
Anger sounds like a child who is not allowed a packet of Smarties.
Anger reminds me of cold, dark winter nights.

Imogen Taylor (10)
Stamford Park Junior School, Altrincham

Happiness

Happiness brings joy to my life,
It's like a rainbow scattered across the sky,
A bird swooping down to its nest,
A furry teddy sat on my bed!

Happiness makes me feel good inside,
The sun shines bright and warms the world,
The flowers grow and brighten every day,
Happiness fills my heart with joy!

Happiness smells like my mum's roast dinner,
Chicken, potatoes, veg, mmm!
Cake, ice cream, jelly, yes please!
This is happiness to me!

Ella Heywood (10)
Stamford Park Junior School, Altrincham

What If . . . ?

My dad calls me Mr Worry,
In fact he says I worry about worrying . . .

What if I have a very bad dream?
What if I don't get picked for the football team?

What if I play badly on the football pitch?
What if I fall down and land in a ditch?

What if I get muddy and very wet?
What if that red jelly doesn't ever set?

What if my friends don't laugh at my jokes?
What if something catches in my bicycle spokes?

What if there's no snow when we go skiing?
What if I don't go up a level in my reading?

What if I don't get my spellings right?
What if burglars break into our house at night?

What if the world ends and there's no light to see?
Where will we go? Where will we be?

What if? What if? What if? I say again,
'Oh no,' I say to Dad, 'I think it's going to rain . . .'

Tom Scotson (9)
Stamford Park Junior School, Altrincham

Anger

Anger sounds like an atomic bomb dropping,
Like a sonic boom!
Anger tastes like the hottest curry,
Like the spiciest vindaloo!
Anger smells like burning gases,
Like rotten eggs when farmers burn their waste.
Anger looks like a crazy bull
Charging at its helpless victim!

Mani Pickston-Bishop (10)
Stamford Park Junior School, Altrincham

Smile!

If you ever see someone with a sad, sad face,
Give them a smile to ease their pain.
It costs nothing to give,
But it is lovely to receive
And you never know when you pass on a smile
Where it could end.
Around the world it could possibly go
As a smile is received, it could be passed on and on,
You never know.

Abigayle Ng (10)
Stamford Park Junior School, Altrincham

Anger!

Anger is like a devil
That follows you around.
He creeps up quietly behind you
And pounces without a sound.

He leaps from a volcano,
All hot and sticky and red,
He isn't ever tired
And never goes to bed.

He comes with no warning
And can spoil the best of days,
And if one plan doesn't work,
He'll find another way.

But never do what he tells you,
For it is probably wrong,
And if you do then you won't be
The only angry person for long.

Siyang Wei (9)
Stamford Park Junior School, Altrincham

Love

Love is as bright as a dove
Flying through the air.
Love is something that
You can take and bear.
Love is the opposite of hate
And love is peaceful and caring,
And loving and sharing,
And it is always around us
No matter what.

Jessica Lancashire (9)
Stamford Park Junior School, Altrincham

Anger

Anger feels like a headache.
Anger looks like a raging bull.
Anger tastes like burnt toast.
Anger sounds like a scream of a frightened child.
Anger reminds me of when they go on about tigers being
                                            eaten and killed.

Laura Sykes (10)
Stamford Park Junior School, Altrincham

Hope

If you don't hope for the best,
The best won't happen.
Hope is like an angel
That guides us and looks after us.
Hope shines through the clouds
Like a burst of light.
It is part of everything we say
And everything we do.
Some people say there is
No point in hoping and believing,
They say hope is a miracle
That will never happen
And if they don't hope, they're right.
If we all hope together
Then miracles will happen
And everything will be all right!

Megan Tamblyn (10)
Stamford Park Junior School, Altrincham

Fear

Fear is terrifying.

Fear clutches at your throat
With a murderous cold hand,
Freezing the blood in your veins.
The dread of walking into darkness
Revealing all worries, stings and pains.

Fear looks like a haunted house,
Inhabited by spiders and rats.
The squeaking of mice and the crawling of lice
And the horrible, ear-splitting screeching of bats!

Fear sounds like the deathly silence
Of a fog-shrouded night on the moor.
Murder most foul, in the shriek of an owl
And the frightening creak of an old wooden door.

Fear reminds me of nightmares,
When you wake up suddenly in your bed,
All worried and shaky, scared and quaky,
But all along, fear's been playing with your head.

Billy Weaver (9)
Stamford Park Junior School, Altrincham

Light At The End Of The Tunnel

Grief, like an abandoned orphan with no one to care,
Confused, yet hoping, though you think it is useless
But it is the only thing you can do,
Like a sludge-green thorn cutting deep into your flesh,
Afraid of the unknown and searching for the truth.
Deep, dark emptiness inside you as you trudge
Through a mournful graveyard full of woe,
Like a toddler screaming in the night, yet no one comes,
Like sparks flying out of the crackling fire and burning you.
Tears of a lonely child come flowing out of their eyes,
A paper cut, sore, like you feel inside.
A weight on your shoulder, a tear in your eye,
Tied down with sorrow that haunts you
In the day, in your nightmares, wherever you go,
Fearing the worst.
But after time, healing makes that important difference,
The piece of you missing becomes smaller and smaller,
Though it will always be there.
Hope, there is always hope.
Hope, though you thought it was useless.
Hope that one day we can live in peace.
Hope that innocent lives of people who are
Far worse off than us aren't destroyed by war.
Hope that your grandchildren will have a better life than you.
Like the light seeping through the emptiness inside,
A chance to start over.
Hope can turn into reality.
Yes, there is always hope,
Like the light at the end of the tunnel.

Harriet Brophy (11)
Stamford Park Junior School, Altrincham

Confusion

A swirling mist,
A laughing man,
You're trying to think
As fast as you can.

Blind as a bat,
As dark as night,
You're trying to think
With all your might.

A cat is wailing
Like a broken violin,
You're turning around
Trying to escape the din.

A fog of colours,
A crescendo of noise,
Your head is pounding,
You see turquoise.

You see purple,
You see black,
Then the pounding
And the noise comes back.

Olivia Whittaker (10)
Stamford Park Junior School, Altrincham

Hate And Love

Hate - the dark, evil poison gas
That floats around overtaking innocent people.
A black monster pulling all those overcome by it into deep depths.
Once hating something, hating gets bigger and bigger,
Like a stone thrown into water and the ripples get bigger and bigger.
Poison flows through the veins piercing the heart eventually
                                        turning it black.
A curse that looms over those possessed by it,
Anger attacks your friends and you find yourself alone.
The Devil himself guides you along the wrong path.
Black destroys light with its soldiers and runs the place
But one little glimmer of light remains filled with hope, faith
                                        and courage.
And now our hero fights off the dark soldiers and stabs them where
                                        they stand,
Taking it upon himself, he attacks the king of darkness himself.
Rays of brilliant white light fill half the room, the other is in the dark still.
Clashes from the couple's swords, white for good, black for evil.
A cry attacks the ruined sight, that of the Devil writhing in agony.
The darkness dims and the light destroys the remains
And now free from this curse the hate turns to . . .

Love

Yes, love is the most powerful guide in the world
So whenever you feel the slightest bit of hate stop,
Or you'll have to fight this battle just told.

Tom Woods (10)
Stamford Park Junior School, Altrincham

Dragons

D angerous, evil beasts, all scaly and red

R anting and raving and waking the dead

A nger raging through the air

G aining speed it finds its prey, catching and eating, it terminates
                                                              his food

O n the horizon it's breathing fire, a bright flaming torch burning
                                                              on and on

N othing can beat this evil thing's speed, I tried it myself but
                                                         never succeeded.

Thomas Elton (10)
Stamford Park Junior School, Altrincham

I'm Angry, Until . . .

My blood is cold,
My face is red,
My eyes are thin,
My palms are sweaty,
My pulse is steadily rising,
My hands are clenched,
My nails digging into myself,

Until she says sorry.

My eyes widen and my fist goes into a hand,
My palms don't sweat,
My face is pale (as usual, that is!)
My pulse returns to a steady rate,
My blood, to room temperature.

'See ya tomorrow!'
We chorus simultaneously!

Meriel Willatt (11)
Stamford Park Junior School, Altrincham

Droplets Of Sorrow

Awakening to a sodden pillow,
Your face far from dry,
Feel shut out from a glorious world,
Feel it's not OK to cry.
All alone, no sound to be heard,
But someone is speaking,
You can't hear a word.
No shoulder to cry on,
No family, no friend,
Your mind is spinning
And you cannot pretend.
You hear footsteps along the hall,
You don't really care,
So continue to bawl.
You peer through your lost mind,
There is a truth that you'll never find.
You wipe the icy droplets of sorrow,
But a voice says
You'll be better tomorrow.

Niamh Adkins (10)
Stamford Park Junior School, Altrincham

Hate

One man walks alone through mist,
His aura a mournful blue.
Alone and uncaring, not noticing
The black shadow which is not his.
At once a shining light pierces the darkness,
A happy man, his aura a bright gold, strides past.
The black beast pounces.
It sinks its evil claws into the sad figure,
Injecting its host with jealousy and spite.
Blinded by the hatred, his aura boiling red,
He strikes out.
Once, twice, then darkness envelopes them both.
The lights go out.

Thomas Christie (10)
Stamford Park Junior School, Altrincham

Hatred

Hatred - when someone blames you,
Your blood boils, burning your insides.

The foul taste of sprouts, all green and mushy,
The horrible smell of burning plastic.

Hatred looks like a bush fire,
Flames spreading through the forest.

It feels like torture paying you back
For all the bad things you've done.

Hatred, growing in your body.

Yacine Meziane (10)
Stamford Park Junior School, Altrincham

Sadness

Sadness - you walk home on your own.
Sadness - you get home, the door is locked.
Sadness - the only way you can get in is the windows.

Sadness - you struggle and slide and you get in.
Sadness - your parents are on the floor,
The lights are off and so is everything else.

Sadness - you call 999 but you're told to hold,
Then two people knock on the door.
It's your sisters, but you don't know, then you answer the door.

Sadness - your sisters walk in then out,
Then the phone rings, you answer, you're not liking it
And then the pitch-black comes over you.

Saskia Palfreyman (10)
Stamford Park Junior School, Altrincham

Laughter!

Bubble . . . bubble . . . bubble, bubble, pop!
An outburst that can't stay in -
Laughter.
Like fizz, fizzing out of a bottle,
As soon as it comes out,
Fizz, fizz, fizz,
Just won't stop,
Like pop, pop, pop!
Fireworks zipping and bursting into colour,
The sun shining above
As the painful silence carries on.
Your mind says, 'Stop! Stop! Stop!'
But your laughter says, 'More! More! More!'
Crackling candy, all different flavours,
And in front of your eyes is shining yellow!
As soon as you start it's infectious,
One person, two people, three people . . .
Everyone!
Laughter!

Nanami Butler (10)
Stamford Park Junior School, Altrincham

Frank Stomp

Once upon a time, in a town on the Rhine,
Lived a guy by the name of Frankenstein.

Now Frankenstein was a bit of a boff,
There wasn't a thing he couldn't pull off.

So Frank said it was his intention
To amaze the world with a great invention.

But he couldn't decide just what it should be,
So he bruised his brain saying, 'Let me see . . .

How about a ship that sails through space?
Or maybe a mask to change your face?

Or perhaps a machine that'll travel through time,
Or a pair of boots that'll help you climb?

Or a flying bike from bits of clocks,
Or a crazy contraption for making chocs?

Nah!' said Frank. 'That ain't no fun,
That's all kids' stuff, it's all been done.

So what will I do to drop their jaws
And bring me their loud applause?

I wonder if,' he mused, 'I can
Put together my very own man

And make him walk and come alive?
Teach him to talk and juggle and jive.

No one's managed that before,
So that's the thing I'll try, for sure!'

So he got two guys with a horse and cart
And he gave them a picture of each part.

He sent them out to find each bit,
Then he worked out how to make them fit.

Legs connected up to feet,
Stick them firmly, nice and neat.

Shoulders need a solid neck,
Stitch and sew and trim and check.

And a head is simply worn in vain,
Unless it holds a working brain.

Imagine a guy three metres tall,
Who's absolutely up the wall!

What will happen, when will it end,
When a monster goes right round the bend?

Then he waited for the next big storm
To wake him up and make him warm.

Then at the very next big crash,
The wire went *fizz* and the eyes went *flash!*

Asim Ditta (10)
Stamford Park Junior School, Altrincham

Happiness

Happiness is the sun shining everywhere,
Blazing down below.
The sky is the colour of dolphins splashing about.
Beaches, warm with people everywhere
Trying to cool down with delicious cool ice cream,
Which melts down their clothes.
Children jumping over the splashy waves
Having lots of fun.
Flowers everywhere surrounding the beach.
Happiness is the sun shining everywhere,
Blazing down below.

Rebecca Sills (10)
Stamford Park Junior School, Altrincham

Hate

Why is it that you wander round
Flitting through the shadows without a sound?
You are like a black vulture
Destroying country and culture.
You prey upon the helpless beings,
Turning the innocent into fiends.
You can infect anybody,
Spreading the poison through the victim's body.
It feels like someone is watching me,
The mists are curling round my knee.

A sound as sharp as a sheet of ice,
The grip as hard as an iron vice,
The hands reach out and take a hold,
No longer are the victims bold.
An emotion as black as coal,
As the evil begins to take its toll.

Thomas Flame (10)
Stamford Park Junior School, Altrincham

Happiness

At times I love to laugh
And love to enjoy the fun,
But when I'm left alone,
I always sit in the sun.

When it's been a hard day,
I'm always proud
Of a long, hard day at school,
Whether it's quiet or loud.

Happiness has a good feeling,
It's whenever you smile.
When you laugh, you're chuffed and proud,
But sadly you can't calm down till after a while.

You can be happy
When you're jolly,
Or happy when you're glad,
So when the rain comes, you put up your brolly.

Nicole Knowles (10)
Stamford Park Junior School, Altrincham

Young Writers Information

We hope you have enjoyed reading this book - and that you will continue to enjoy it in the coming years.

If you like reading and writing poetry drop us a line, or give us a call, and we'll send you a free information pack.

Alternatively if you would like to order further copies of this book or any of our other titles, then please give us a call or log onto our website at www.youngwriters.co.uk

**Young Writers Information
Remus House
Coltsfoot Drive
Peterborough
PE2 9JX**

(01733) 890066